Talking Treasure

Stories to Help Build
Emotional Intelligence and Resilience
in Young Children

Vered Hankin   **Maurice J. Elias**
Devorah Omer   **Amiram Raviv**

Illustrations by Nurit Yuval

RESEARCH PRESS
PUBLISHERS

2612 North Mattis Avenue ■ Champaign, Illinois 61822 ■ [800] 519-2707 ■ www.researchpress.com

RESEARCH PRESS
PUBLISHERS

Copies of this book may be ordered from Research Press
at the address given on the title page.

Composition by Jeff Helgesen
Illustrations © Nurit Yuval
Cover design by Linda Brown, Positive I.D. Graphic Design
Printed by Seaway Printing

ISBN: 978-0-87822-672-6
Library of Congress Control Number 2012931919

Contents

Foreword

Stories make our lives meaningful. They put together individual actions that may not mean much at first but mean a great deal when viewed from the perspective of the story. So too do they convey that life can sometimes be a struggle, but even the greatest obstacles can be overcome. Such an insight develops resilience in a child, demonstrating that our lives have meaning, for stories illustrate a sense of wholeness, with a beginning, a middle, and an end.

Vered Hankin and her coauthors have written an insightful book that can serve as a guide to teachers, storytellers, psychologists, and lovers of folklore. *Talking Treasure* demonstrates the deep psychological meanings of stories, giving vivid examples. Dr. Hankin, herself a storyteller and psychologist, has drawn on her knowledge of both fields in equal measure, with remarkable results. She and the other authors make the case that stories can serve as guides to the inner lives of children and are tools of immense healing potential in working with them.

Above all, this book is a practical guide to understanding the profound meanings of stories, as well as how to use them to communicate meanings intended to build resilience and self-esteem. *Talking Treasure* deserves to be widely known among those who have long sensed that stories and storytelling are keys to understanding many of life's mysteries.

—HOWARD SCHWARTZ
PROFESSOR EMERITUS,
UNIVERSITY OF MISSOURI–ST. LOUIS

Introduction

Did you like listening to stories when you were a child? It's rare to find anyone who did not. Do you remember your favorite tales? Can you remember who told you the stories? When? Where? Again, most people can.

Stories help us make sense of the world. Stories give us hope when we feel down; they give us wonder and excitement when our lives seem ordinary; they help us find fairness in a world that sometimes seems unfair. The stories we listened to as children helped us deal with all the confusions of life that we experienced growing up.

Life throws a great deal at children that they find hard to understand. Conflict between people, people hurting others, people hating others, people threatening others—children encounter stories with these themes on the Internet, during the evening news on television, and in other media. What are we telling our children about the stories they receive from these sources? What messages are we giving them that there are positive things in the world, and in themselves, that they can count on?

We—their parents, teachers, and other caregivers—are the strongest influences on children. As we know from our own childhoods, stories are an excellent way to help children think about and better understand the world around them. More than that, stories help children look ahead with confidence to a better world that they can help create as they get older. Life is made up of many stories, but we have to add our voices clearly and read stories to our children that will help them understand the world and how to find their way through it.

This book is meant primarily for children between the ages of four and eight, although some three-year-olds will love to listen to the stories. Likewise, some children who have had the stories read to them when they were younger will pick up the book and read the stories themselves again when they are nine or ten. Younger children approach all the stories with a great sense of wonder. They particularly relate to "The Horse Who Thought She Was a Puppy," "The Day the Children Became the Parents," and "The Night the Toys Were Left Alone." Older children find that "The Girl Who Never Lost," "When Mr. Pot Cracked," and "David and the Spider" touch a special chord inside them. And all children seem to love "The Talking Treasure," "The Apple Tree's Wish," "The Reed and the Wind," and "The Four-Eyed King." The multiple layers in each of these stories offer various levels of complexity, effectively providing a different story for each developmental stage.

The stories in this book are timeless. Some are original; others come from many lands and cultures and exist in many versions and various languages. When stories come from other sources, we have added to them in subtle but important ways, keeping the bones of the stories intact. Our purpose is to enrich the stories by providing supplements, just as one would add vitamin supplements to one's diet. We have also modernized some of the stories to reflect the tastes of today's children. These stories are "child tested." They have been told to children numerous times, in different ways, until we were able to find the right balance. Research has taught us a great deal about how to help children become more emotionally intelligent as they grow up. We know that children with low "EQ," or emotional intelligence, can experience higher levels of depression and anxiety than their peers, even when they exhibit high IQs. We have added important activity and discussion suggestions to the stories to help develop your children's social and emotional intelligence. Specifically, the "Parent and Teacher EQ Guide" that follows each story helps parents and teachers get a little extra out of each tale and assists children in finding their own "treasure chest"—their inner thoughts and feelings. In this guide, we first take you "Inside the Talking Treasure" to give you some insights about the meaning of the story. We also point out some of the personal connections that children might make in the story, to help you understand why they may be reacting strongly, or in certain ways that might surprise you, to some of the themes as you are reading. Next, "Exploring the Talking Treasure" provides questions to help children think about the story and how it applies to their lives. These questions will also help sharpen children's emotional intelligence skills and will probably suggest other questions you could ask, as a dialogue develops with a child or group of children. Finally, "Spreading the Talking Treasure" includes activities so that the themes of the story are not only heard but also experienced, expanding children's emotional intelligence. Although many of the questions in the "EQ Guide" refer to "your child," these stories have been written with teachers and other caregivers in mind. They are intended to contribute to the development of resilience in children, whether they are your own children or students in your group or class. Of course, you can just read the stories without following the suggestions in the "EQ Guide." It's up to you!

Though the stories are meant to be fun and joyful, they are also grounded in a rich psychological tradition. One of the important contributions of dynamic psychology is directing attention toward the internal world that each of us possesses and that affects our lives and guides much of our behavior. Emotional intelligence emphasizes that, although many emotions exist in our consciousness, others are outside our level of immediate awareness. These emotions may become accessible to consciousness with some effort and motivation. Stories are particularly important windows to this internal world. As children (and adults) learn to be sensitive to their own and others' emotions (which happens as they listen to the stories), they (and those reading to them) gain an increased awareness of the range of emotions they are experiencing. At the same time, children become more sensitive to the emotions of others.

The importance of empathy in everyday life to the functioning of our households, classrooms, and schools is not always appreciated. Empathy involves "trying on someone else's shoes" and seeing things from his or her point of view. Children's discovery of empathy is a formative experience in their developmental process. The building blocks begin in infancy, toddlerhood, and the preschool years. As children move through early childhood and into the preteen years, they become aware of having insights into others and themselves that enable a fuller and more complex experience.

Developing a sensitive, complex, and rich personality is an ongoing process that demands educational investment. Children need to learn to understand how to voice their feelings. They must be taught ways to cope successfully and when and how to reach out to others when they are down. Once they are comfortable with these skills, they will grow up to be more confident, have better relationships, and be more likely to achieve success in school and in life. This is a large part of what it means to be emotionally intelligent.

Reading stories and discussing the characters' motives and emotions is just one way of enhancing emotional intelligence. Open and honest conversations with children, accepting and nonjudgmental references to their emotions, and adult modeling of willingness to open up and disclose emotions are additional means of developing self-awareness and other emotional intelligence skills.

At the end of the book, in an appendix, we include some more background about emotional intelligence—what it is, exactly why it is important, and how it has been built into the stories. It is not necessary to read this material to gain the benefits of this book. It is included simply for those of you who are interested in further ideas and insights to better understand yourselves and your children.

The Talking Treasure is waiting to be opened. In it, ten stories await. They will amuse, serve as sources of wonder, soothe and calm, provide hope, and teach skills that will help children learn to cope with life's ups and downs. As any parent, teacher, or other caregiver who reads to children realizes, a really good story does not simply end with the final "happily ever after." It lives beyond the words on the printed page in our thoughts, feelings, and memories. It is our intention that many of your fondest wishes for your children—that they grow up to be caring, thoughtful, creative, responsible, loving, and involved people—will be supported through the stories of this book. These will indeed be moments your children will treasure for a long time, in ways that will be powerful and profound.

The Talking Treasure:
Expressing One's Inner Feelings

Veronica woke up feeling strange. No, it wasn't the flu, or even a cold, and really nothing hurt. Veronica wasn't quite sure what it was, but she just woke up with this strange sense. She wasn't sure what to do about it or what to say. So she just said nothing. She got up as she always did, at the same time she always did, brushed her teeth, got dressed, and went outside to play, but somehow nothing was fun on this day, and this strangeness kept hanging on.

"Maybe I just need to walk a bit," Veronica thought. And so Veronica did. As she began to walk, she began to feel better. Her feet briskly moved her about, but every time she slowed down, the strangeness returned. So Veronica sped up, and **sped up,** and **SPED UP!** Soon she was zipping so fast, she wasn't even sure where she was going. She just had to shake this feeling! She walked and walked and walked and walked until…

Veronica's feet started to tire. She looked around. Hmmm…she found herself in a beautiful forest. Why, she didn't even know there was a forest around here! But, there, right there, was a beautiful big tree, with a perfect trunk to lean against. Veronica did just this and fell into a deep sleep.

"Wake up! Wake up!" Veronica was startled by a little screechy voice. She looked around but didn't see anyone. "Right here!" the voice called out again. Veronica looked down. There he stood, the smallest man she'd ever seen. Why, he must have been no bigger than the size of her thumb!

"Who are you?" she asked, curiously.

"My name is Little Voice. And I guess you can hear why. But everyone calls me Little V."

"I can see why," Veronica said with a smile.

"I have come here to give you a surprise."

"A surprise?!?" Veronica lit up. She loved surprises!

"Can you pleasepleasepleaseplease tell me what it is?" (Does this sound familiar?)

"Well, you see, it's a very important present. You must take very good care of it."

"Oh, I will! I will!" Veronica promised.

Little V lifted a box, a tiny little box. It was about as big as Little V, and so Little V could barely carry it, but for Veronica it was just a tiny little thing.

Veronica looked curiously at the tiny little box. "What is it?"

"This, Veronica," Little V announced, "is a talking treasure."

"It is?" Veronica's eyes widened. "What does it say?"

"How do I know what it says?" Little V replied, impatiently, waving his arms. "It's not my treasure!" And with that Little V and the forest disappeared, and Veronica found herself back in her bed!

"Wha...?" Veronica was confused.

"Veronica," she heard her mother's voice, "your breakfast is getting cold. Time to wake up!"

Immediately, Veronica jumped out of bed. To her very big surprise, she was still clutching the talking treasure. "Am I dreaming?" she wondered. But then she heard something. "You were a little scared," it whispered, "and confused. It would be so nice to get a hug from Mom!"

"Wow," Veronica thought, "that is just what I was feeling!" She ran into the kitchen and gave her mother the biggest, best hug ever. Just then her brother rushed in. "Hey, Justin, you won't believe what happened today!" Veronica began.

"Sorry, squirt, no time. Gotta go to soccer practice." And Justin ran out.

"Your feelings are hurt," the treasure chest whispered. Veronica looked down. It was true! Wow—just to hear the talking treasure say it, she felt a bit better.

"Veronica," her mother called her in. "Your teacher told me you did very well on your book report. I'm proud of you, and I made your favorite chocolate pudding to celebrate!"

"Ah…" the talking treasure chest whispered. "That sure feels good to hear, doesn't it?" Veronica looked at it, impressed. Again, it was exactly right! She thanked her mom and ate all of her pudding!

All day long, Veronica kept the talking treasure with her, and every time she felt something it would tell her what it was. She no longer felt strange. Somehow that feeling just passed, and Veronica was having fun exploring how different things made her feel! She felt sad when a butterfly flew away, excited when she saw a bunny, and a little bit nervous when the lights went off for bed. The talking treasure would whisper each of these to her, and Veronica would feel better just knowing somebody knew how she felt.

But the next morning, Veronica woke up feeling strange again. She wasn't sure why, but she knew it was there. She waited for the treasure to tell her what it was. But she didn't hear anything. She looked around but she didn't see anything. The talking treasure chest … it was … gone! Veronica felt terrible. Where could it be?

She began to search everywhere, her entire room. But she couldn't find it. There was only one thing left to do. She began to walk. She walked and she walked and she walked, until … finally … she reached the forest. She couldn't quite find the same tree, but she found a similar one and leaned on it until she fell asleep.

"Wake up! Wake up!" Veronica heard Little V say.

"Oh, Little V!" She called out happily. "I am so glad to see you! I lost the talking treasure. I don't know where he went. Can you help me? Please?"

Little V began to laugh. He laughed and laughed and laughed.

"What's so funny?" Veronica asked angrily.

"You didn't lose it!" Little V laughed. "It's impossible to lose it!"

"No, I really did!" Veronica sadly insisted.

"Don't you see?" Little V asked. "Did you ever open the treasure?"

"Why, no," Veronica said.

"Did it feel heavy?" Little V asked.

"I don't know, but you had so much trouble lifting it up! It had to be full!"

As Veronica said this, Little V took a blade of grass and started to lift it, pretending to have the most difficult time possible.

"You see, I just allowed you to think there was something in the treasure chest. Really, everyone has the talking treasure all the time. It's inside of them. I just helped you see it a bit more clearly. But it's always been with you and it always will be."

"Really?" Veronica lit up. "Well, where is it?"

"Inside," Little V replied. "You see, sometimes we feel our feelings very strongly, and they leap out at us, like when something hurts so much we just start crying, and we can't stop it no matter how hard we try. But a lot of times, there are little feelings, and they happen all the time. Sometimes we hear them, sometimes we don't. And if we don't listen for a while, well…we can start to feel a little strange."

"That's it! That must be that strange feeling I had!" Veronica tried to listen, but she didn't hear that whisper. She didn't hear much of anything. "What if I don't have a treasure inside me?"

"Sometimes it's harder to hear the treasure," Little V explained. "Those times, what you can do is close your eyes, maybe put your hand on your stomach, and feel your stomach rise and fall as you breathe, nice and steady. Then imagine you are somewhere far away, peaceful, and picture yourself on a trip with … well … yourself! Then just ask the kid in your mind what she's feeling or what she wants."

Veronica tried it. She closed her eyes, put her hand on her stomach, and began to breathe as steady as she could. At first she had all kinds of thoughts and worries, but she continued. She imagined herself in another place, by the ocean, and could see the waves rising and falling. She asked the girl in her mind: What do you want? And that's when she saw it. The girl was sitting alone, looking sad.

"Oh!" Veronica exclaimed. "Could it be that I've been feeling a little lonely? Well, that does seem right…"

"And don't forget to keep listening…" Little V called out, as the forest faded and Veronica found herself—back in bed!

She stretched out, leaped up, and ran outside to the playground, but not before giving her mother a huge hug, and picking up her kitty to take with her so that she wouldn't feel alone. But Veronica didn't feel so alone anymore. No. She knew she had the talking treasure deep inside of her, whenever she needed it.

Parent and Teacher EQ Guide

 ## Inside the Talking Treasure

As our first and title story of the book, "The Talking Treasure" helps children see how important it is for them to learn to recognize and express their feelings. Our feelings allow us to connect with other people—the treasure of good relationships—but we have to give voice to those feelings, usually by talking about them or expressing them in other ways. The talking treasure inside all of us is our ability to recognize how we are feeling and express it to others.

In this story, Veronica discovers her talking treasure, or what has been described by some as her "inner voice." Veronica learns that if she listens carefully, she can identify her inner voice. She also finds that listening to her inner voice helps her to be more sensitive and attentive to the emotions of others around her. When she gives her mom a hug and picks up her kitty, she will find that her mom is more likely to give her hugs and her kitty is more likely to pay attention to her and want to be with her.

Sometimes children are surprised that the talking treasure is useful in ways other than helping them identify their own feelings. The talking treasure provides children with words that enhance their self-esteem and give them confidence by reminding them how important some of their quieter needs are. As we appropriately help children develop their vocabulary of feeling words and hear adults' words describing their strengths, we give children powerful tools to build a strong sense of self and to make a difference for the people in the world surrounding them.

 ## Exploring the Talking Treasure

1. What did Veronica dream about?

2. What did Little V give Veronica as a present?

3. Why couldn't Veronica find the talking treasure?

4. What did Veronica learn at the end of the story?

5. Can you remember some dreams that you have had? What were they about?

6. If you had a talking treasure, what would it say to you? What would it say that was good about you?

7. What do you do when you are feeling strange or sad to help yourself feel better?

8. How can you tell what other children or adults are feeling?

 ## Spreading the Talking Treasure

1. Even though children often don't speak their feelings aloud, they may feel down or lonely. Sometimes we get so busy that we may not be aware of this, even in our own children. Try to check in with your child every day, especially around new events or transitions. By providing a listening space, you can help your child find that his or her talking treasure speaks a bit louder and clearer.

2. Watch a TV program with your child, then ask your child to try to describe what the different characters are feeling. If he or she has trouble, try using slow motion to see the characters' faces more clearly. Do the same thing by looking at the pictures in books your child is reading.

3. Does your child have a place to put special things? If not, ask if he or she would like one and what he or she would most want to put in there. Consider setting up such a place, using simple materials.

4. Talk with your child about what you think is special about him or her.

5. Help your child draw pictures of various emotions, including happiness, sadness, fear, and so forth.

6. Ask your child to tell you about the kinds of things that make him or her happy. While you are driving in the car, ask your child to tell a story about someone that has happy things happening to him or her.

7. Have your child draw and tell a story about a child (or animal) that has sad things happen to him or her, and what he or she does to cheer up.

8. Share a memory from your childhood with your child and ask for his or her reactions.

9. Ask your child to join you for a moment in holding hands. Invite the child to close his or her eyes. Guide the child to listen to his or her breath for a moment. Can your child feel the breath moving through the body like a wave? Then ask, "If you had a talking treasure inside of you, what might it be saying? What do you think it is feeling right now? What does that emotion feel like in your body? Take another couple of breaths and open your eyes. How do you feel now?"

The Horse Who Thought She Was a Puppy: A New Family Member Arrives

Once, long ago, a horse sat in her stable on a small farm. Because the farm was small, with very few animals, the horse had a stable all to herself. There she could stretch out and eat as many oats as she could ever want. In return, the horse had to work, to carry heavy things for her master and grind corn at the mill. Still, the horse did not complain and enjoyed serving her master. She also enjoyed being the only horse in the barn. The master's daughter would always pay her special attention and make sure to brush her mane until it was shiny as could be.

One day, the master of the farm brought home a special treat for his daughter: a new puppy! The whole family was so excited! They all watched the puppy, laughing, as he scurried about, wagging his tale. Every chance they had, they would give the puppy a treat, pet him, kiss him, and call him over so he could jump onto their lap.

Everyone thought the puppy was adorable. Well, everyone except for the horse. For weeks after the puppy joined the family, no one paid any attention to the horse at all. The only time anyone came into the barn was to let the horse out to do her chores. Meanwhile, the puppy had no chores at all. The horse watched him through her window, and the only thing the puppy had to do was lie around on his back looking happy and contented so people could rub his belly—or run or jump or try to catch things.

The puppy also had special eating privileges. He got special puppy treats, and sometimes even snacks from the family's table! And while the horse did have her stable all to herself, the puppy slept inside the house with the humans! All this infuriated the horse. After all, she had been there much longer! Shouldn't she be the one getting all the attention?

When another week went by without a single visit from the master's daughter, the horse began to think, "It's not like it's so hard to do the things the puppy gets rewarded for. He just sleeps, runs around, licks people, and eats. But he could never do the things I do! And why do I have all these chores when he has to do nothing but just look cute? It's really not fair!" The more the horse thought about this, the angrier she became…

Until, finally, she had a brilliant idea! "If they want someone to roll around and jump about, I can do that! I can do everything he does! If that's what they like, I'll do it, and they'll think I'm just as cute as he is, if not cuter!" The horse pushed and pushed until finally she broke free from the stable and galloped into her master's home! There, to the shock of her masters, she began running around in circles, just as she had seen the puppy do. Unfortunately, instead of looking cute, the horse was so big that she began accidentally knocking down her master's fancy artwork and pottery. "Stop!" the mistress of the house called out. But the horse knew just what to do. She had seen the puppy do this many times, and it always worked. She leapt over toward the mistress so she could jump onto her lap. The mistress let out a blood-curdling scream. "Our beloved horse is attacking me!" she cried out. The horse was very confused. All she wanted to do was cuddle as she had seen the puppy do so many times. But somehow it just wasn't working.

"They just don't know how cute I can be," she assured herself, and immediately she knelt down, rolled onto her back, and exposed her cute little belly so they would come over and rub her stomach, just as she had seen them do with the puppy so many times. The whole family walked over to her carefully. "Here they come!" she thought, excited. "Aren't I cute?"

"Wow," her master sighed. "I guess our horse must be very sick. I've sure never seen a horse act quite this way. If she doesn't get better, we may have to take her away to the doctor or maybe even the animal hospital."

When the horse heard this, she grew terrified. She didn't want to go to the hospital! Why, she loved it where she was! Carefully, she scrambled onto her feet and galloped back to her stable.

That night, she didn't sleep very well. She kept worrying that maybe her owners would send her away. Oh, why couldn't she have been happy just being a horse instead of trying to be like a puppy?

In the morning, she heard someone coming. "Here they come," she shivered. "It's all over now . . ." But, to her surprise, it wasn't her owners at all, but the puppy!

"Umm . . . Sorry to bother you, but I saw the barn door open. I always wondered what it might be like out here," the puppy said shyly. "You get your very own little house. And you get to run around in the field, too. They always make me go out on a leash. Would you mind showing me around?"

At first the horse was not so happy to see the puppy, but soon she and the puppy were running around and playing. They ran around all morning, until finally the two of them cuddled together and fell asleep for a long nap. When they awoke, the horse couldn't believe it: The family surrounded the two of them, saying, "Here they are! We were so worried! Look at them! Wasn't it nice of our horse to show the puppy how to gallop in the field? She must be feeling better. Wow, cuddling together like this, they both look just adorable!"

From then on, the horse was happy and content to have the stable all to herself with as many oats as she could ever want and a list of chores that only she could do. But most of all, she enjoyed having a new friend around. For although the two of them were very different, they knew they would always be best friends.

Parent and Teacher EQ Guide

 ## Inside the Talking Treasure

It can be hard for adults to understand how children feel when someone else receives more attention than they do. Think about times in your life when this happened to you. Perhaps it was in school, at work, among your friends, or even in your own family. This may give you some idea about how children feel when a new sibling enters the home. Sibling rivalry is not new, of course. It has been captured in ancient stories, including those of the world's major religions.

The story uses animals to show the feelings of jealousy and deprivation that even the most secure individual can feel when suddenly confronted with unexpected competition. A new visitor joins the family. A visitor who is not required to do any chores, who is not obliged to contribute to the family, and who receives a lot of attention and pampering, placing the older tenant in the shade. The horse in the story wonders, as do children in the same situation, what she did wrong that led to the need for a puppy to be brought into the household.

The story illustrates in a humorous fashion the horse's futile attempt to behave in a way she thinks is appreciated. Her main error is not realizing that expectations for her and for the new puppy are very different. In her jealousy, she also fails to realize the advantages she is given due to her age and status. The threat (usually exaggerated) directed at her helps the horse realize her mistake. The story teaches children some very important lessons:

- It is important to be happy with what you have and with who you are.

- Very often, harmony and cooperation lead to better results than conflict.

- Children have value as they are and need not become like everyone around them.

- Children can learn a lot from those who seem different from themselves, including that they may have more in common than it seems on the surface.

These insights can be applied not only to relationships within the family, but also to relationships among children in general, so the story is not limited to siblings.

Exploring the Talking Treasure

1. What did the horse think when she saw the way everyone was behaving with the new puppy?

2. How did the horse feel when nobody was paying attention to her?

3. What would you think about a horse that behaved like a puppy?

4. Could the horse have been jealous of the puppy? Why?

5. What did the puppy think, and why was he jealous of the horse?

6. When was the horse smarter, in the beginning of the story or the end?

7. Can you explain the expression "Be happy with what you have"?

8. Are there any times that you felt like the horse? What about the puppy? What happened and how did you feel?

9. In what ways were the horse and puppy alike? How were they different? What did you learn from the horse and puppy about how people can be the same and different?

 Spreading the Talking Treasure

1. Have your child draw the stable and a doghouse next to it.

2. Ask your child to make up a story (that you write down) about a cow that had an older calf and then gave birth to another calf, and what happens next. See if your child would change the story if the animals involved were lions, whales, or monkeys.

3. Find a song about brothers and sisters and see if members of your family can learn the words or music or at least hum or play along in some way.

4. If your child has a brother or sister, ask your child to think about the things they do together that are the most fun. Try to find a time every day, or almost every day, when they get a chance to do one of these things, even for a short period of time.

5. Ask what things a brother or sister does that bothers your child the most. Ask how he or she tries to get the brother or sister to stop. Would your child do the same thing with an older or a younger sibling? Ask what your child can try that might work better.

The Four-Eyed King:
Overcoming a Disability

Once a long time ago, way up high among the tallest of mountains, there lived a family of eagles. This family was not just any family. They were the king and queen of the eagles, and they lived with their son, the little baby eagle prince. Now the king of the eagles had a very important job. His job was to use his super-eagle sight to locate food from far away. All of the birds in his kingdom would follow the eagle king so that they, too, could share in the meal. The eagle king also would stay up all night guarding the birds, and whenever he saw a dangerous animal approaching he'd call out, "ALERT!"

The eagle king served the birds for many years. But as the years went by, he began to grow old. Soon he found that he lacked the strength and energy he used to have as a young king. One day, he pulled his son aside and said, "My son, I have served the birds as king for many years. It is now your turn to follow in my footsteps. Tomorrow at this time, we will hold a special ceremony for you. You will lead the flock to food and then you will be named the new eagle king!"

Well, the eagle prince was so excited! Now that he was no longer such a little eagle, he was ready to rule the birds! He looked at his father with great pride, thinking, "Wow, can I do it? Can I be as great an eagle king as my father? I sure hope so! I will definitely give it all I've got!"

The next day, all of the birds of the kingdom gathered together. They surrounded the eagle prince, chirping to one another with pride. "Well," the eagle king announced, "you all know that today is a very important day. I am too old to lead you, but I have great faith in my son. He has watched my work, and I have taught him everything I know. I am certain he will lead you well."

Everyone looked at the eagle prince with anticipation. The king announced, "And now, before we grant him his official crown, he will lead us all to our dinner!" The little eagle prince knew just what to do, for he had watched his father many times. He spread out his wings and took off, with all the birds following. He floated up and down, just as he had seen his father do. Each time he rose, and each time he fell, the birds followed closely. That's when he saw it! Down below, there it was! A huge fish! "Wow," thought the prince, "it might even be a whale, it's so big!"

Immediately, he began zooming down, with the birds behind him. He zoomed all the way down and caught the fish in his talons. But, wait a minute! This was no fish! This was—a dog? Yes, the eagle prince had mistakenly landed on a sleeping dog—and the dog was pretty angry about being woken up! The dog began to growl and soon began barking loudly, snapping at the birds with his teeth. Swiftly, the eagle prince leapt into the air, with the birds safely following. Whew! They made it safely! But what exactly had happened? "Why would the eagle prince lead us to a dog? We certainly do not eat dogs!" the birds whispered to each other. "This is all too strange!"

Once the birds landed, the prince felt so ashamed he could barely face his father. He just didn't understand what had happened. He had never seen his father make such a mistake! "Never mind," his father comforted him. "You will try again. And when you succeed, I am certain you will be a very fine king." The prince felt a little better, but he knew he must try again. The very next day, the prince was ready: "One, two, three…go!" he called out as he spread his wings and floated off into the sky, searching for some prey. One by one, the birds followed him, their stomachs still empty from the night before. Just then, the eagle prince saw it! Mmmm…it looked yummy and juicy— a giant squirrel! It was so big it could feed the whole village! He began to zoom all the way down, with the birds following right behind him, their beaks watering as they got closer and closer. Then, ta da! The eagle prince landed swiftly and elegantly, with the birds right at his heels. But, alas! What happened to the squirrel? The eagle prince had landed on a mailbox! As the birds landed they had to dodge the cars that were coming their way, and once again they all returned without supper.

When they returned to the top of the mountain, the eagle prince felt even more ashamed. "I guess I wouldn't make a very good king, huh?" he asked his parents. "Maybe someone else should be king instead of me." A teardrop fell from the prince's eye.

"There, there," his mother soothed him. "I know you are disappointed. But, sweetie, can you explain to us why you chose a dog and a mailbox to land on when you knew neither would be very tasty?"

The eagle prince bowed his head and slowly raised it. "Well," he said, "you see, ummm…"

"What is it?" his father asked. "Whatever it is, you can tell us."

"You won't be mad at me?" the eagle prince asked tentatively.

"We'll sure try not to be. What is it, honey?" his mother inquired worriedly.

"Well, the truth is…I…I…don't see very well. I mean, when things are farther away…I'm sorry I didn't tell you earlier. Then you would have known not to pick me as the eagle king. I mean, who ever heard of an eagle who can't see well, let alone an eagle king?!?"

The eagle king spread out his wing and wrapped it around his son. "Son," he said softly, "I have flown all over the world and I have seen many things. You know, in the human world I have seen very important people, even presidents, who can't do a lot of things. But they make up for it in other ways."

"They do?" the eagle prince looked confused. "How?"

"Well," the eagle king replied, "for example, they don't have hard nails and sharp beaks like we do, but they use knives and scissors to cut things. They don't have wings like we do, but they build airplanes so they can fly. They don't have fur or feathers to keep them warm, but they make clothes to cover them during the cold winter."

"Really?" the eagle prince looked up. "But... how can those things help *me*?"

"Well, there's one other thing that many of them don't have. Some of the most important humans, even their presidents, even their kings, often have trouble seeing, just like you."

"They do?" the eagle prince said, surprised.

"They sure do. And you know what they do about it?"

"What do they do?" the prince asked eagerly.

"They wear glasses!"

"Glasses!" the eagle queen exclaimed. "Of course, how brilliant! We will get you a pair of glasses!"

Indeed, not too long after, the king and queen gave the eagle prince his very own pair of glasses. While the eagle prince was worried that perhaps the other birds would laugh at him, he was pretty excited to be able to see. At first, some of the birds called the new eagle king "Four Eyes" behind his back, but on the day of his ceremony to become king, he captured so many different kinds of food that every one of the birds ate enough for a whole week. Afterward, they all took a post-dinner nap in some bushes, while the newly crowned eagle king kept watch far above on top of the mountain. As he sat proudly, he suddenly spotted a tiger slyly inching its way toward the sleeping birds. "ALERT! ALERT!" he called out in his best kingly voice, waking all the birds just in time for them to fly away to safety.

The birds were so grateful to the new eagle king for saving their lives and for the wonderful meal that no one ever dared make fun of him again. They continued to call him "the four-eyed king," but not to make fun of him. They wanted everyone to know that it would take at least two of any other king to measure up to their four-eyed king, who was the best king they ever had.

Since that time, there have been many eagle kings. But only one of them, a very special eagle king, was the famous Four-Eyed King, and he was never forgotten.

Parent and Teacher EQ Guide

 ## Inside the Talking Treasure

This animal fable speaks to our ability to overcome physical challenges. Near-sightedness can be fixed by wearing eyeglasses. But wearing glasses makes the person's disability visible, thus making that person stand out. The discovery that a child needs eyeglasses might initially affect his or her self-esteem. Children are usually intolerant of differences and might react with rejection and ridicule. Wearing eyeglasses is but one example of a relatively common disability.

The story has two objectives: to help stigmatized children deal with self-esteem issues and to help them deal with being ridiculed by peers. The story emphasizes the utility of acquiring instruments for coping with the disability despite the fact these may reveal the handicap and lead to stigmatization. But there is also a broader purpose to the story: to promote children's tolerance of persons with disabilities, to try and equip them with empathic skills, and to encourage them to attempt to understand the strange and different instead of rushing to judge, reject, condemn, or ridicule.

The use of the eagle, known for being sharp-eyed, as the character who needs glasses provides an ironic and somewhat humorous point, emphasizing that weaknesses can be found even among the best of the best. The same point is also emphasized in the arguments brought by the king and queen, which tell about respected humans who wear glasses, too, thus showing that having a disability does not necessarily harm a person's status.

 ## Exploring the Talking Treasure

1. Why did the eagle prince want to give up the role of king?

2. What did the birds think about the prince's clumsiness and "misses?"

3. What did the birds think when they saw the prince wearing eyeglasses?

4. What can we learn from the story?

5. How does a child feel when he or she first starts to wear eyeglasses? What are the hardest things to get used to about wearing glasses? Do other people help or make it harder to get used to glasses?

6. Do you know children or adults who have been in a similar situation? How did they deal with it?

7. What do you think about a child who looks different from other children? What problems do you think he or she faces in school and other places? How can you help?

8. If a child looks different from other children, how do we know what kind of person he or she really is?

9. What was most helpful to the Four-Eyed King in learning to live with his problem? Who or what helps you to deal with problems you are having?

 ## Spreading the Talking Treasure

1. Ask your child to tell a story about a different or exceptional child that he or she knows. As part of the story, make sure your child talks about ways he or she is different from, but also the same as, the exceptional child.

2. Have your child draw a picture of different or exceptional children and tell a story about them (try not to use the child discussed in the previous activity). As part of the story, be sure your child talks about ways he or she is different from, but also the same as, these children.

3. Ask your child to try to imagine and tell a story about what would happen if he or she went to school in another country. How would your child get along if he or she were different from all the other children?

4. See if your child can try to imagine, and possibly draw or create models of, inventions that might help people with different kinds of disabilities. Perhaps your child can think about how to make public spaces like airports, train stations, libraries, food stores, movie houses, and big stores easier places for people with different handicaps to manage.

5. Ask your child to name presidents, kings, queens, and other leaders. Go to the library or use the Internet to look up some information about them and talk about what made them good leaders or not-so-good leaders.

The Apple Tree's Wish:
The Beauty Within

Once, a long, long time ago, there was a little baby apple tree. Bit by bit, as little apple trees do, this apple tree began to grow. And as it did, each night its eyes would wander up to the sky. Now, hovering above this apple tree there was a giant oak tree. The oak tree was so big that its branches seemed to reach to the sky. Indeed, between the oak tree's branches, the apple tree could see the stars in the sky, twinkling. But to the apple tree, it seemed that the stars were actually part of the oak tree's branches. "Wow," thought the apple tree, "I hope one day I have stars too, just like the oak tree. Yes, one day I, too, will have stars!"

The apple tree continued to grow and grow. Seasons came and went. Springtime came, and the apple tree blossomed. All the other trees looked at the beautiful apple tree with its flowers, and the apple tree was happy.

But at night when the stars would come out, the apple tree looked up toward the oak tree. The apple tree saw the beautiful stars in the oak tree's branches, and the apple tree wanted, more than anything, to have stars just like those. "Please," the apple tree called out to anyone who would listen. "Please! Can I have stars? Can I have stars, too?" But all the apple tree would hear is just the rustling of the branches, the whistling of the birds, the clicking of the crickets, and the hooting of the owls.

Soon, summertime came and the apple tree grew apples: big, juicy, beautiful, tasty apples! All the other trees looked at the apple tree admiringly as its fruits hung proudly for everyone to see. The apple tree was very proud!

But at night, when everything was dark, the apple tree looked up, and there—there—were those beautiful, glistening stars! "Pleeeease!" the apple tree called out to anyone who would listen. "Pleasepleasepleasepleasepleaseplease!!!!! I want stars too, just like the oak tree! Why can't I have stars? It's the only thing I want! It's not fair! Please?!?" But all the apple tree would hear is just the rustling of the branches, the whistling of the birds, the clicking of the crickets, and the hooting of the owls.

The apple tree tried to be patient, but night after night, there was that giant oak tree, taunting the apple tree with its beautiful stars! Each night the apple tree begged, wishing with all its might: "Pleeeeease?!?" but all the apple tree would hear is just the rustling of the branches, the whistling of the birds, the clicking of the crickets, and the hooting of the owls.

One night the apple tree called out, "I beg of you, please! I want staaaaaaaaaaaaaars!!!" When the apple tree heard no response, it couldn't take it anymore. "Fine! Fine! You won't give me stars! It's the only thing I want, and you won't give me stars! I'll never have stars…" The apple tree was angry and sad. It curled up its leaves and began to cry. It cried and cried for all those days and months and years of wanting stars. And as it cried, its branches began to shake. They shook and they shook. They shook and they shook. They shook and they shook and they shook and they shook until … kaboom! One of the apple tree's apples fell and broke into two!

"Ohhhhhhhhh!" the apple tree cried. "Now I've lost one of my favorite apples. My most scrumptious, superbly delicious apple!" But just then the apple tree looked a little closer. It looked a little closer, and it looked a little closer, and … there it was, before it! It seemed to the apple tree that the apple had something right in the middle! Yes, could it be … a star!?!

You see, the apple tree had stars inside it all along. It was too busy looking at the oak tree to notice its own beautiful stars. And so it is, that if you cut an apple into two, after first turning it to its side, you too will find a star in that apple. And stars just like these—well, not exactly these, but only a little different—are inside of you, just as they were inside of the apple tree's apples. You don't even have to cut yourself open to find them. All you have to do is to believe they are there.

Parent and Teacher EQ Guide

 ## Inside the Talking Treasure

Children today live in a world of temptations. They are exposed to many others who seem to have more, bigger, better, or newer things. No sooner do children get a new product than a new model is on the market. Sometimes this leads to jealousy, possessiveness, and a desire to obtain what others own, even if what one already has is sufficient. This creates a tension between one's need to develop and achieve more and one's self-acceptance and appreciation of what one has. When children do not appreciate what they have inside them and instead always look around for something "better," feelings of sorrow and frustration are very likely to arise.

Self-esteem is acquired at a young age and develops throughout the years as a result of children's achievements, and the reactions of others—mainly parents—to them. Children who feel loved and appreciated by their parents and teachers grow up to be children who learn to love themselves and appreciate what they have. However, children who do not receive such attention may continually search outside of themselves for a sense of worth and satisfaction.

The apple tree desperately wished for what the oak tree seemed to have. For parents, teachers, and children, the story reveals how frustrating it can be to be obsessed with what others have. The moral of the story is very old and warns of the dangers of ignoring the happiness at home or within oneself. Such a moral can be found in other stories, such as *The Blue Bird*, a play by Maurice Maeterlinck about two children who search the world looking for the blue bird that represents happiness, only to find the bird nesting on the doorstep of their home.

It is important for children to develop a sense of appreciation for what they have and to find contentment in that. This allows them to have a better sense of balance in our culture, helps them cope with feelings of jealousy, and highlights the importance of being happy with one's share in life.

 ## Exploring the Talking Treasure

1. Why did the apple tree want stars?

2. What was the apple tree unhappy about?

3. What was special about the apple tree?

4. What did the apple tree eventually discover?

5. Where did the apple tree keep its stars?

6. Did the oak tree really have stars?

7. What happens when you want something that somebody else has and you don't? How do you feel when this happens? What is an example of this and what did you do about it?

8. What makes you special?

9. What do you have that you think others would like to have? Think about not only what you own, but also who you are as a person, and your relationships with other people.

 ## Spreading the Talking Treasure

1. Ask your child to draw a tree with big apples on it. On each apple, have the child write or draw something that shows a special treasure in his or her life.

2. Take a walk with your child at night. Look at the stars. Try to count them. When you come in, ask your child to draw some big stars in the sky and write or draw something someone else has that is very special. Then talk about how nice it is for that person to have this thing, and how nice it is that your child has special things also.

3. With your child, find or make up a story about a child who has everything anyone could want. Say what those things are, and be sure to include in the story what might happen if the child never stops trying to get more and more things.

4. When you are in the car or taking a walk with your child, ask if he or she would like to trade something with a friend who has something he or she wants. What would your child want to give the other child in return?

5. Ask your child to imagine an "inner star" and what it would look like. Then have your child draw it and show it to others.

The Girl Who Never Lost:
Taking Risks

Is it true that there really was once a girl who never lost? She never, ever lost a game? She never came in last in any competition? It may be hard to believe, but there really was once such a girl, a girl who never ever lost.

This girl, she wasn't the strongest or the fastest or the wisest person in the world. No, she was just an ordinary girl who woke up every morning, brushed her teeth, got dressed, brushed her hair, ate her breakfast, and went to school. Just like all the rest of her classmates, she went to class, ran outside during recess, and came home from school. At home, she would do her homework, eat dinner, read, use the computer, and sometimes watch TV. Each night, she would head to sleep and sleep well, waking up ready for another day.

There was, however, one big difference between this girl and other children. What was it? What was this special trait that caused her to never, ever lose? Well, you see, she never played board games or video games. She never played sports or even cards. In fact, she never played, well, anything at all! While other children played, she simply watched. Whenever her school held competitions—science fairs or spelling bees—she never participated. Even in gym class, she would always excuse herself by explaining that her knee or her ankle hurt, or perhaps she had a headache. That way, she never had to try. She wouldn't even participate in simple games such as marbles or rock-paper-scissors. No tic-tac-toe, not even solitaire. Whatever the game was, she simply sat out.

Now this may sound strange to you. Why would a perfectly healthy girl never play a single game, not inside or outside, not in the morning or at night, not at school or at home? Why, you ask, why??? Well, because…because…she was afraid…afraid…of losing. "What if," she thought, "what if I don't even get one point in the video game? What if I get last place in a race? What if I let my whole team down in a game of sports? What if I lose in a game of checkers, chess, or cards? Would it mean I am…well…a loser? Maybe it's better not to try at all!"

And this was the girl's secret—the reason she never, ever lost.

But you see, this very same girl, although she never lost, she never won either. And sometimes, when she sat at home watching others through her window as they laughed and joked and played, a little voice inside of her would wonder, "It does look like fun. What if I did try? What would happen? Would it be possible…that even if I didn't win, maybe…just maybe…just the game…might be…fun?"

Parent and Teacher EQ Guide

 ## Inside the Talking Treasure

One of the most famous quotes in sports is "Winning isn't everything; it's the only thing." The philosophy behind this quote reflects the difference between teaching our children the importance of achievement and competition and teaching our children that only winning is acceptable. As we see, the story demonstrates the price paid by an ambitious and anxious girl who values only winning. She avoids confrontation, avoids new things, and therefore never loses. But the unavoidable consequence is that she also never wins, and the price that she pays is boredom, not being involved in teams and many groups, and a lack of challenge in her life.

To learn how to win, it is also important to learn how to lose. Learning to lose is a developmental process that requires time and educational investment. It is important to teach children that if you want to win, you must also be willing to risk losing. The message is that although you may lose an activity, a game, or a competition, you do not lose yourself—you are not a failure. Learning can be rewarding and playing can be fun even without winning, especially when it leads to growth, building skills, and increasing capabilities. Children benefit from learning that they can survive even if they don't win.

 ## Exploring the Talking Treasure

1. Would you like to be friends with a girl like the one in the story? Why or why not?

2. If you knew a girl like this, what would you advise her to do?

3. Is this girl happy? What is she happy about? What isn't she happy about?

4. How do you feel when you win? Why is it good to win?

5. How do you feel when you lose? Why don't you like to lose? Can you think of a time when it was not so bad to lose? Tell about it. Is there a time you can remember when you did not win but you felt proud of yourself? Tell about that time.

6. Is it possible to win all the time?

7. How would you feel if you had someone in your class who always wins?

8. How would you feel if you had someone in your class who got angry whenever he or she loses? What would you like this person to do instead of getting so angry?

Spreading the Talking Treasure

1. Plan a game in which it is impossible to lose, perhaps by changing the rules of a board game so that everyone wins. How does it feel to play this way?

2. Change the rules of a board game or card game so that the person who does the best, who would normally win, in this case loses. Games like Chutes and Ladders, Candyland, Sorry, and Uno work well for this, as do card games like rummy, casino, go fish, or even war.

3. Ask your child what games he or she most likes to play with friends and why. If your child isn't sure, or even if he or she knows, have your child ask the friends about their favorite games and why they like them.

4. Encourage your child to work with other children, and yourself if necessary, to make up a story with the title, "The Longest and the Worst Game Ever." It can be a lot of fun to keep this story going over a period of a few days.

5. Encourage your child to talk to family members and make a list of everyone's favorite games. Try to remember to play these games more often during family visits and holidays.

6. Play a card game in which you change the rules and the idea is to lose, not win. Good games to try are card games like war, casino, go fish, gin rummy, and even poker.

The Reed and the Wind: Strength in Flexibility

Once, a long time ago, there was a reed that swayed by the river. For the most part, the reed was happy, swaying to and fro, but once in a while, when the wind would blow, the reed found itself swinging helplessly to the rhythm of the wind. At these moments, the reed would gaze admiringly at a nearby oak tree, which stood firmly rooted to the ground. No matter how hard the wind blew, the oak tree remained straight, tall, and firm. "Hmmm," muttered the reed. "If only I could be as tough and strong as that oak tree. I would stand my ground and no one could move me in any direction! That lucky oak tree…"

One day, the wind woke up in a very bad mood. She began to shake and spatter and rumble. "Oooooh!" cried the wind. "Whoever gets in my way today, I will take with me, so watch out! Ooooh!" The reed began to shudder, but the oak tree stood firm.

"Ha!" cried the oak tree. "I am not scared of you! I am too powerful! I will not budge! I will not move out of your way, and you cannot take me with you!" The oak tree's words made the wind very angry. With all her might, the wind shook the oak tree's leaves and branches, and a few of the branches broke off in fear, to join her. The reed looked on terrified, but the oak tree stood firm.

"I won't move! Go on your way!" bellowed the oak tree. "Humph!" the wind groaned. With a giant gust, she twisted her muscular arms under the oak tree's roots, and with one colossal "Hiyah!" she swooped up the oak tree, flinging it into the air.

"Uh-oh!" the reed trembled. "If the wind could uproot the oak tree, what could she do to me? I am so little and frail. Oh, no, here she comes!" And before the reed could say "Uh-oh!" one more time, the wind shifted directions and began blowing right onto the reed! The poor reed had no choice but to follow. The wind shook the reed to the right, and the reed followed right. She shook the reed left, and the reed followed left. The harder the wind shook, the quicker the reed followed, until soon the two were dancing.

"Ooooh!" exclaimed the wind. "When I swing to one side, you swing with me. When I swing to the other side, you swing with me, too. Wherever I swing, you swing. Instead of fighting me, you listen. You understand." The wind slowed down, until finally she came to a whirling stop. Then she drifted away, calmer than ever, lightly humming, "Ooooooh…"

The reed remained in its place, swaying back and forth, just as it always had. "Hmmm…" thought the reed. "I guess things aren't always what they seem. Maybe I'm not so weak after all! Maybe there is strength in swaying back and forth. I may even have made a friend!"

Indeed, from that day on, whenever the wind whirled through, she would slow down next to the reed, bow her head, and extend her arms for a dance.

Parent and Teacher EQ Guide

 ## Inside the Talking Treasure

Through this story, we see how important it is to listen to others rather than always insisting on having our own way. We all like to get our way and might even prefer to have it our way all the time. But living with other people, who also want to get their own way, means we have to wait our turn sometimes. Other times, it takes special character to join with others and work together rather than always try to have things go exactly the way we want them to.

Although we want our children to be flexible, we may worry that they will not make thoughtful decisions, choosing simply to "follow the wind." Don't we want our children to be strong in their opinions like the oak tree? While the oak tree and the reed are both strong in their opinions, it is important to note the wisdom of the reed. The reed knew how to resist the wind, even dance with the wind, without ever shifting its ground. We want our children to grow up with the emotional intelligence to deal with all kinds of people, with many opinions and points of view, but also to stay rooted in the values that are most important. By being able to see its similarities with the wind, the reed kept from being blown away by because of its differences. But while the reed was able to move with the wind, it never lost its roots. For children, the message is important but subtle: You should be willing to listen to others and compromise as long as your values are not being threatened.

Children must know their values and be clear about what is most important in their lives. Young children learn this from watching and listening to trusted adults around them. For parents and teachers, having conversations about character, morality, and guiding principles to live by are necessary because children receive many mixed messages from the media and from peers. Flexibility is important. Children can learn how to be flexible like the reed, to "roll with the punches" while at the same time understanding and honoring that there will be times in their lives when they will want to keep true to their deepest beliefs, even when the wind blows very hard the other way.

Exploring the Talking Treasure

1. How did the reed feel about the oak tree at the beginning of the story? How about at the end? Why did the feelings change?

2. How did the reed feel about the wind at the beginning of the story? How about at the end? Why did the feelings change?

3. What did the oak tree say to the wind at different parts of the story? How do you think the wind felt about what the oak tree was saying? What did the wind do to the oak tree and why? How could the oak tree have spoken differently to the wind and maybe not have gotten uprooted?

4. Ask your child to think about a time when he or she was like the reed and another time when he or she was were like the oak tree. What happened? How did things go? Would things have gone better if he or she had been a little more like the oak tree or a little more like the reed in either of the situations?

5. Go back and reread the part of the story where the oak tree stands up to the wind:

> "Ha!" cried the oak tree. "I am not scared of you! I am too powerful! I will not budge! I will not move out of your way, and you cannot take me with you!" The oak tree's words made the wind very angry. With all her might, the wind shook the oak tree's leaves and branches, and a few of the branches broke off in fear, to join her. The reed looked on, terrified, but the oak tree stood firm. "I won't move! Go on your way!" bellowed the oak tree.

Ask your child how the oak tree actually said these words to the wind. Have your child role-play to show you and emphasize that the oak tree was too challenging, too direct, and too threatening. Then ask your child to role-play saying the same words in ways that might not have gotten the wind so angry (for example, by paying attention to posture, tone of voice, and eye contact while speaking). A less aggressive way of speaking can sometimes lead the same words to have a better effect.

6. Ask your child to think about things that are actually stronger and more long-lasting because they are flexible. Some examples include suspension bridges, tall buildings, airplane wings, swords, the pyramids in Egypt, lids on the covers of everyday food storage containers, and rubber bands. You can probably think of many others! Combine this discussion with an activity to show how some of these are flexible, even though they may not appear that way on the surface. Help your child understand that in dealing with other people, relationships can be stronger and more lasting when there is some flexibility. You can also ask your child, "Are there times that you feel more like the oak tree? Are there times that it feels right not to give in like the reed?" Help him or her see that in any of the examples presented earlier, too much flexibility means a loss of integrity, in all senses of that word.

 ## Spreading the Talking Treasure

1. Have your child draw pictures of the story as a comic strip, summarizing the action in four or five scenes.

2. Give your child a blank piece of paper and some crayons, markers, or colored pencils. Have the child fold the paper in thirds. Ask the child to use colors and designs to show the feelings at the start of the story, the middle, and the end in each of the three parts of the paper. Have him or her share the drawings with family members or other children; talk about reasons for choosing the feelings depicted. (You may need to reread the story first and help your child decide what he or she sees as the beginning, middle, and end of the story.)

3. Have your child write or role-play some conversations between the oak tree and the wind that lead to different endings. How would your child change what the oak tree said? What might lead to the best story ending for the oak tree? For the wind? For the reed?

4. Ask your child to pick some songs that go along with the story, sing them, and talk about why they seem to match the story well. You may need to help investigate some books or recordings of children's music.

5. Ask your child if he or she knows someone who is a lot like the oak tree. Like the reed? Like the wind? Help your child find a time to talk to these people and share the story with them.

6. When the family is together at dinner or some other time when there are not many distractions, start a conversation about what is most important to you, a conversation about the values and the character traits that you are most proud of. You can decide whether to ask your child to react, respond, or share what is most important.

When Mr. Pot Cracked:
The Beauty of Imperfection

O nce, a long time ago, when people wanted water, they could not just turn on the tap or twist the knobs on the shower or press the button on the drinking fountain. Once, the only way to get water was to walk all the way to the well. The well was very deep, and you would need to throw a big bucket down the well with a rope around the handle. The water would fill up the bucket, and the bucket would become very heavy. Then someone would have to pull, pull, pull the bucket up, up, up out of the well. Not everyone could do this because it was a very difficult job. But people needed water, and so every village had at least one water carrier, someone whose job it was to go fetch the water out of the well. Usually, the water carrier would carry two very large buckets or pots filled with water back and forth from the well to the town. It was a tough job, yes, but it was also very rewarding. After all, what more important job could someone have than to supply people with their most basic need—water?

Garvey was the water carrier of his town. He had been the water carrier for many years, and he had watched many children in the town grow up. He had seen many things and spoken to many people and was respected by all. Every single day, he would trudge out to the well with two very large pots. He would fill the two pots to the rim and carry the water about the neighborhood, selling some to each of the neighbors. Then he would head back to the well, several times a day, until finally it was time for him to turn in for the night. After all, he needed his sleep for another day of work!

One night as Garvey was sleeping, his pots, the very pots he carried every single day, began whispering to each other. "Did you notice how much water I carried today?" Ms. Pot asked, puffing up. "Did you notice how full I was?"

"Yes, you did pretty well," Mr. Pot conceded. "But I have to say I was pretty full myself. I'm certain the villagers drank their full in large part because of me!"

"Oh, you think so?" Ms. Pot retorted. "I don't think you're quite the pot you think you are."

"What does *that* mean?" Mr. Pot raised his voice.

"I'm afraid, Mr. Pot, that your place among the rest of the pots will not last long. You, my friend, are cracked."

"Agh!" gasped Mr. Pot, and then he fell silent. After a few minutes, Mr. Pot sheepishly looked up. "Um, you were just being mean, right? I'm not really cracked, am I?"

Ms. Pot looked down, ashamed. "I'm sorry I said it in such a mean way, but…I'm afraid you are. Look!"

Mr. Pot looked down, and indeed there was a thin but noticeable crack running down his side. "What good am I?" Mr. Pot began to wail. "A cracked pot! Poor Garvey has to work so hard pulling up the water, and then I probably leak it all out!" All night long, Mr. Pot could not sleep. Instead, he just cried silently to himself, and little teardrops slid out through the crack.

The next day, Garvey woke up early as he always did. He lifted Mr. and Ms. Pot over his shoulders, as he usually did. He began walking the long way toward the well. As he walked, Mr. Pot was shaking and shivering, feeling terrible about his crack. Should Mr. Pot tell Garvey? After all, if the water leaked out, Garvey would have to make twice the trips to the well! Just then, they arrived at the well, and Garvey grunted as he slowly and strongly pulled up the full pots of water. He lifted the heavy pots over his shoulders and began on the path back to the village.

Mr. Pot tried soooo hard to hold the water inside, but soon the water began trickling out of the tiny little crack. Mr. Pot felt soooo bad. He finally couldn't take anymore, and so he called out "Garrrvvvvveeeeey!"

Garvey turned toward the pot. "Mr. Pot, what is it?" he asked, concerned.

"Oh, Garvey, I'm so sorry, but I'm no use to you anymore. I hate to tell you because I'm sure you'll throw me out, but…but…well…I have a…crack! I'm leaking!" Mr. Pot covered his ears, terrified at what Garvey might say.

"Oh, Mr. Pot!" Garvey shook his head, smiling. "Is that what you're worried about?"

Mr. Pot slowly nodded.

"Don't you see?" Garvey asked. "Mr. Pot, look down the path as we walk."

Mr. Pot looked down, though he could barely stand it, and he saw the water spilling out of the crack. "By the time you get to the village half of my water will be gone!" he exclaimed.

"Oh, Mr. Pot," Garvey said, calmly, "you're not looking closely enough. Yes, the water is spilling out, but look where it's going." Mr. Pot looked down on the ground, and he could barely believe his eyes. Along the path, there was a beautiful trail of flowers, rising up just where the water was falling. "If it wasn't for you, Mr. Pot, we wouldn't have these beautiful flowers along the path. Every morning as I walk down this path, my day is brightened as the flowers smile to me, lighting my way. And others in the village feel the same way. We think, thank goodness for Mr. Pot!"

Even Ms. Pot, who heard the whole thing, had to admit that a piece of her wished that it was she who had a crack, just like Mr. Pot. That night, all of the pots in the house honored Mr. Pot for being the most special pot, the only one who could create a trail of flowers for all of them to appreciate as they walked down the long path home.

Parent and Teacher EQ Guide

 ## Inside the Talking Treasure

Self-esteem is acquired over a period of many years, and it affects the manner in which we perceive our world and environment; consequently, it also affects our behavior. The process of seeing oneself in a positive way begins early in childhood. As part of developing self-esteem, it is natural to compare ourselves and our characteristics to those of other people. For many children, the comparisons begin with their siblings. For others, it begins when they enter day care or preschool or kindergarten and first grade. Even young children realize when others can do things better than they can. And it is natural for them to feel uncomfortable as a result of what they perceive as shortcomings that they find in themselves. We may try to change the things we are unhappy with, but some things are very hard or even impossible to change. Furthermore, sometimes it may not be in our best interest to change because not everything that is different about us is necessarily bad. In fact, those things are often the ones that make us so special and unique.

This story is based on times children look around and think, "Everyone is better than I am." This person is taller and that one has more games. She runs faster, and he can tie his shoelaces without any help. It is about how someone can be different, and even think he or she is not as good as everyone else, but still be quite special. It is important that we help our children, and all children, find their special qualities and focus on the good they bring into the world. No matter how seemingly small it may be, a quality can still be special and important in ways we can't always see and understand. Finding and appreciating that special quality can offset many perceived shortcomings.

 ## Exploring the Talking Treasure

1. How did Mr. Pot feel in the beginning of the story? In the middle? At the end?

2. What got Mr. Pot so upset?

3. What happened when Mr. Pot told Garvey he had a crack?

4. If you were Garvey, what else would you have said to Mr. Pot to make him feel better?

5. Do you have a special toy or doll that has a crack or a small piece missing? How do you feel about it? Does it matter that it has something wrong with it? Have you ever had a toy that was more special because of something that wasn't quite perfect about it?

6. What do you think is special about you? If you had to tell someone what is special about you, what would you say?

7. What is something about you that you would like to change? It might be very small, like a very small crack, but still be something you would like to change. How can you do it? How can others help you to do it?

 ## Spreading the Talking Treasure

1. Take a piece of colored paper and, with your child, use it to make a list of what is special about your family or your child's school or classroom.

2. Help your child draw some pictures that go along with this story. Some possibilities include the following:

   ▪ How Mr. Pot and Ms. Pot feel at the end

   ▪ Mr. Pot's surprised look when he realizes all the good his crack created

   ▪ How proud the other pots are of Mr. Pot at the end

   ▪ Garvey hauling water

   ▪ Garvey and Mr. Pot when Mr. Pot tells him he is worthless

   ▪ The flowers that Mr. Pot's crack helped to grow

3. Talk with your child about someone in the family who is not doing well or feeling down. Plan something your child can do to reach out and help the person feel better. Use questions like these to get the conversation started:

   ▪ Have you ever felt down?

   ▪ Have you ever felt like you wish you could be like someone else?

- What made you feel better? Is there someone in the family who is feeling sick?

- What are some things you could say or do to make them feel better?

4. Encourage your child to talk with parents, grandparents, other relatives, teachers, and other adults in school about special toys, games, dolls, and so on that they had, where they got them, how long they lasted, what happened that led them to give up these things (if indeed they have), and how they felt when they gave them up. You will probably need to take an active role in helping a younger child have these conversations, but you will probably get a lot of insight out of them yourself!

5. Take one or more magazines you no longer need and help your child cut out pictures of 20 or 30 different people. Then ask your child to sort the pictures into piles that are made of pictures that are similar. What do the people in each pile have in common? How are the ones in each pile they made similar to each other and different from those in the other piles? Next, you may ask your child to sort them into piles that are made of pictures different from the others. Ask what makes each pile different, but also ask them what is similar about the ones in each pile. These questions, connected to a hands-on activity of working with a set of pictures, will help your child see that our differences also include similarities. You may even help your child label the similarities as things that are "special."

The Night the Toys Were Left Alone: Dealing with Separation

One evening, Mommy and Daddy were getting ready to leave for a play. They were dressed up in fancy clothes, Mommy in a beautiful long dress and her favorite pearls, and Daddy in a nice, crisp suit. They gave a good night kiss and a warm hug to little Isabella and her brother Luis, showed the babysitter where the toys, books, and snacks were, said goodbye, and headed for the door. After some games and some bedtime stories, the babysitter whispered goodnight, turned off the light, and closed the bedroom door.

That's when it happened. Just as the lights went out, the toys began to cry. Teddy the bear sniveled, Dolly the doll whimpered—even Silly the happy clown was fighting the tears in his eyes.

"Why are you crying?" whispered little Isabella. "Teddy, you're almost old enough for school. Dolly, you're a smart little doll. And you, Silly, I'm very surprised at you. A clown with tears in his eyes? What is all this about?"

But the poor toys couldn't help it. It was dark—and the toys let out a wail. "We're scared of the dark!!!" cried Truckey the truck.

"It's different when Mom and Dad are here! I want them to come back!" the coloring book bawled.

"Waaaaaaaah!" they all cried out at once.

"What are we going to do?" Isabella asked her big brother, Luis. "How can we make them feel better? Mom and Dad will be home soon."

But the toys refused to listen. "They left us all alone!" Teddy called out.

"Yeah!" chimed in Dolly. "We're all alone now. We're scared…"

"Don't worry," Luis said to the toys. "Isabella and I are here to protect you. You're not alone."

"We miss them!" the toys cried out. "Bring them back!"

What could Luis and Isabella do? They got out of bed and tried playing a game of make believe; they put on their favorite CD; they even snuck into the play room to turn on cartoons, but nothing worked. The toys continued to cry and cry.

"What would make you feel better?" Isabella asked.

"Well…" sniffled Silly the clown, "we could maybe call them."

"Call them?"

"Yes! Call them! Call them now!!!!" the toys all cried out together, sniffling and crying, crying and sniffling.

"That's impossible!" Luis called out. "If they knew we were awake we would be in big trouble!"

"But they left us all alone!!!" they cried.

Isabella and Luis looked at each other, about to give up. Isabella was not sure exactly why, but she was starting to feel a little sad, too. What if the toys were right? What if they were truly alone? And when would their parents come back? It seemed like they would be waiting forever!

Just then something caught her eye, a shimmering light from the window. "Hey, look!" Isabella suddenly exclaimed. "Look outside! The moon looks almost full!"

"You know what?" Luis chimed in, "I see him. It's Grandpa Moon, the grandfather of all the stars. At night he comes out to keep watch on all the stars out there and also on all of the kids and toys whose parents left them alone. That's his job. You know, sometimes when Mommy and Daddy leave I look outside and search for Grandpa Moon. Look: You see, he's looking at us! He's even smiling a little bit!"

"Yeah," Isabella agreed. "It's true. I see a little bit of a smile!"

"Really?" Dolly looked up.

"Could it be?" Teddy asked.

The toys searched through the sky. There, smiling widely, was Grandpa Moon and his grandchildren, the stars, stretched out as far as the eye could see.

"I think he winked at me!" Silly the clown exclaimed.

One by one, the toys stopped crying. Silly got his smile back. Teddy cuddled up to Isabella. Dolly went to sleep. Truckey parked. And all the paints and blocks and coloring books went back into their cubbies.

From then on, the toys never cried again when Mommy and Daddy left. Whenever they felt afraid, they just peeked outside. Even with Mommy and Daddy away, they would never again feel completely alone. Grandpa Moon would always be watching.

Parent and Teacher EQ Guide

 ## Inside the Talking Treasure

Young children sometimes become frightened and worry that their parents will not come back when they leave. This is normal from a developmental perspective. Young children respond most strongly to what is directly in front of them. The saying, "Out of sight, out of mind" is very often true for young children. When they don't see their parents, they may wonder whether they will be coming home or if they even still exist. This does not happen all the time, of course. A very good babysitter may distract children so their minds are occupied. However, sometimes even the best substitute caretaker is not enough for the child who misses his or her parent or primary caretaker.

Here, the story takes a twist by having the toys rather than the children get upset when the parents leave. The toys give voice to feelings that many children have. In the end, the children find a way to soothe the toys (and themselves) so that they feel reassured. Even though it may not make a lot of sense to adults that the moon can be a source of comfort and protection inside a home on earth, many children find the idea very comforting.

 ## Exploring the Talking Treasure

1. How were the toys feeling when the parents left?

2. Why do the toys need the presence of parents?

3. Have you ever felt scared of the dark or scared of being alone?

4. What might help stop the toys from worrying so much?

5. When you look at the moon, what does it look like to you?

6. Does the moon ever look like a grandpa to you?

7. When you are feeling sad or scared or lonely, what do you do that helps you feel a little better? What other things help you feel better?

Spreading the Talking Treasure

1. Before you go out and leave your child with a babysitter, leave behind something that is yours. It can be a key, a handkerchief, or anything that will help your child to remember you and serve as something you will be sure to come back for. Teachers who know they are going to be absent can do the same thing with their preschool through third-grade classes, and this will help children be calmer and behave better with substitute teachers.

2. Have your child draw a picture of the moon. After that, use a computer or a book to show your child pictures of a full moon. Then, ask your child to draw the moon again. Have him or her point out what is different the second time.

3. Tell your child that sometimes it will be cloudy and he or she will not be able to see Grandpa Moon or the stars. Have your child draw a picture to keep and look at to help him or her feel safe on a cloudy night.

4. Play a game where your child gives books, toys, games, and other possessions alliterative names like those used in the story— for example, Larry Legos, Paula Pillow, CD Sam, Dora or Donald DVD.

5. Watch any of the movies in the *Toy Story* series. In those movies, the toys come alive and have feelings just like the toys in this story. After you watch the movie, reread this story and ask your child how in what ways the story is similar to and different from the movie.

6. Play a game of hide and seek with your child or create a scavenger hunt where you hide some everyday items where they can be found without too much trouble. When you have finished, ask your child what the word *hide* means. Make the point that things that are hidden are not gone— they are just out of sight. Explain that when you go someplace, you are out of sight for a little while, but just like the items in the game you

played, you come back and can be seen. The next time you are going to be away for the day, or even just a few hours, remind your child that you will be back, just as if you were playing a hiding game.

David and the Spider: Everyone Has Value

Once, a long time ago, when King David was just a child, he was afraid of spiders. Spiders looked so big and icky to him. He loved all animals, but spiders—with their big long legs and sticky webs—he could do without. One day, when he grabbed his toy sword from the back of his closet, he was surprised to run into a sticky web. Out crawled a big brown spider, startling little David. "Achh!" he let out before he could keep it back. "A spider in my closet?!? Of all things! I wish there weren't spiders in the world at all. What good are spiders for, anyway?" Suddenly David felt brave. "I should crush you!" he announced.

"Oh, please don't do that!" he was surprised to hear the spider plead, in a small screechy voice. "I promise that one day, I'll show you how important spiders can be."

David stepped back, laughing: "Spiders? Important? I don't know about that! But since you asked so nicely, I will save your life. But you must never startle me again!"

"You won't be sorry…" the spider screeched as it scurried away.

Time passed, and little David grew older. He became a very brave young man, never afraid of anything at all. In fact, though he was smaller than many other men, he became a very famous soldier. When no one else could beat a great giant, David knocked him down with only a slingshot.

Because David fought so well in the army and was respected by all of the other soldiers, the ruling king became jealous of him. He was afraid that David would want to take his power. People started whispering that the king wanted to find David and put him in jail. "David! David!" they warned. "You'd better hide! Quick!"

David began to run. He ran and ran into the hills, until finally he reached a deep dark cave. He could hear the king's horses galloping his way, and so he quickly ducked into the cave, crawling in as far as he could go.

The galloping sound grew louder and louder until it came to a halt—right outside David's cave. The king's soldiers were standing just a few feet away from the cave! Surely they would find him! "You, search near the river!" the general commanded. "And you, search all the nearby bushes and trees!"

David's heart was beating, for he knew that any moment they would check the cave and all would be lost! "Sir!" he heard one of the soldiers. "Look at this! A cave! Shall I search inside?" David's heart stopped as he waited breathlessly for the soldiers to find him.

But to David's surprise, the general replied, "No use checking the cave. Look, there is a spider web covering the entire entrance. If he had gone in there, he would have surely broken the web. Onward!" the general commanded, as the soldiers climbed upon their horses and galloped away.

David let out a deep sigh of relief. He looked around, saw the spider, and, when he looked very closely, realized it was the same spider he spared as a child. David turned to the spider and whispered, "You saved my life."

"I did," the spider screeched. "I told you that you wouldn't be sorry and that you would see how important spiders really can be!'

"You were right," David smiled. "I learned something today. Spiders are very important. All of the creatures of the earth are, even if I may not always know how. And I promise, if I become king, that I will never forget this."

Because of the spider, David did eventually become king of the land, and even though he promised he wouldn't, once in a while he would forget his promise and find himself a little nervous around spiders. But whenever King David found himself beginning to stiffen up, he'd hear a screechy voice calling, "You'll see...!" Then he would remember the spider that saved his life, showing him the importance of all of the creatures on earth.

Parent and Teacher EQ Guide

 ## Inside the Talking Treasure

Young children naturally think of themselves as the most important people on earth, with the occasional exception of their parents and teachers. As they get older, most children come to understand that others' feelings and perspectives matter, and many extend their concern to the world around them and learn (if they have received the necessary modeling and instruction) to care about the environment.

However, nowadays, because of media and societal messages, children continue to think of themselves as more important than anyone else. When this happens, they are not considerate of the feelings of others, and they are not always kind or concerned about the world around them. As children start being cared for out of the home at younger and younger ages, it becomes more and more important for them to learn that, although they are very important, so are others around them. This story helps children realize that even a king, a very powerful person, can owe his very life to a spider. If not for the spider, the king would surely have been caught. The other lesson of the story is that not only is the seemingly lowly spider clever, the spider also does not hold a grudge. Even though the king insulted the spider, the spider helped the king. Children can learn from this that everything has special qualities and that showing forgiveness can help others, and themselves, in unexpected ways.

In a related way, this story helps teach children that they should be careful about making judgments about others based only on appearances, and certainly not on the first impression alone. There was much more to the spider than David had initially thought. We can never tell when someone's inner treasure will be important in our own lives. This story helps children appreciate the world around them, all aspects of nature, and how important even small things—like webs and spiders—can be to our lives. As David learned, such an understanding can help develop humility and put our own importance in a better perspective.

Another important point of the story is that everyone is afraid sometimes. Even David, who grew up to be king, was afraid—first of spiders and then of the former king. He may have been brave enough to fight a giant, but he had his own fears to overcome and his own lessons to learn.

 ## Exploring the Talking Treasure

1. Ask your child how David felt about the spider at the beginning of the story and how he felt at the end. Also ask how the spider felt at the beginning and the end of the story.

2. Why did the soldiers leave without looking into the cave?

3. Why did the spider make a web in front of the cave?

4. How did David feel when the soldiers went away? How did he feel when he saw the spider web and the spider?

5. Ask your child to pretend that he or she was the spider. Would he or she have made the web to save David? Why or why not?

6. How do you think David will treat the people of his country when he becomes king? Why do you think so?

7. What are some benefits we receive from spiders?

 ## Spreading the Talking Treasure

1. Share with your child a time someone did something wrong to you and you forgave that person. Tell your child how you forgave the person and what the person's reaction was, if any.

2. Ask your child to share with you a time he or she forgave someone who did something wrong, as well as times when he or she did not forgive. Have your child talk about times he or she is willing—and unwilling—to forgive.

3. Help your child make a drawing, poem, or song that tells the moral of the story.

4. Find some different kinds of music that your child likes to listen to. Ask your child to find a song that seems to fit with the mood at different times of the story. You may need to help your child by first reviewing the way feelings

change as the story unfolds, on the part of the spider as well as David. Compare the different songs and artists chosen and ask why the particular choices were made.

5. Go outside with your child (or look in an encyclopedia or on the Internet) and point out the activities of small insects and what they contribute to nature (for example, small plankton feed on small sea creatures, which then feed the fish that feed us). This will help your child see the interconnection of many things in the world—what some refer to as the circle of life.

6. Tell your child about a time you felt afraid and how the situation was resolved. Ask your child if he or she has such a tale to share with you.

The Day the Children Became the Parents: Developing Empathy and Appreciation

It was Sunday afternoon. Just like any other Sunday, Daddy sat in his chair reading his paper and drinking coffee. Mommy was reading a novel. Little Amy was playing quietly in her playpen. Everyone did what they always did. That is, everyone except for Amy's big brother, Matthew. Matthew already created a castle out of blocks. He already put together all his puzzles. He even played for hours with his trucks. Now Matthew was bored!

Suddenly, Matthew had an idea! "Hey," he called out. "I know a game we can play! Mommy, Daddy, could you play a game with me—please?"

Daddy looked up from his paper. Mommy looked up from the book. "What's the game?" they asked.

"It's a game I just made up! How about we trade places! The kids will be the parents, and the parents will be the kids! Daddy, give me the newspaper and the coffee. Mommy, give Amy your book! Here, Daddy, you take Amy's pacifier. Isn't that so cute! Such a big boy with a pacifier! And get up, young man—this is Daddy's chair, my chair, not yours!"

Before Mommy and Daddy knew what was happening, Matthew put Daddy into the high chair and Mommy into the baby carriage. Matthew dressed little Amy in one of Mommy's big dresses and put Mommy's shoes on her little feet. He took some lipstick and put it on little Amy. Then he ran to get Daddy's coat, briefcase, shoes, and keys.

Poor baby Amy was scared. She wasn't sure what was going on! But Matthew scolded, "Mommies don't cry! That's enough crying now. We have a lot of things to do!" When Daddy wanted to watch his favorite news show on TV, Matthew wouldn't allow it. After all, it's not for children! Matthew turned off the TV and took away the remote control. Then he called his parents—that is, the kids—for dinner. "Dinner is served! Right now! Not in a minute! Not later! NOW!"

Mommy began to complain that she didn't really like porridge, but Daddy Matthew wouldn't hear it. "It's good for you!" he commanded, and made little Mommy eat each drop of Amy's porridge.

Little Mommy wanted go on a stroll outside in the baby carriage and happily, Daddy Matthew that she could. Oops! But then he remembered that he had work to do and he couldn't go out after all. "Don't cry, baby!" he said. "What's so terrible? We'll take a walk another day!"

Then he looked at little Daddy. "And don't you worry," said Daddy Matthew. "I promise when I'm done with my work that I will sit you on my lap and I'll tell you all about what I was like when I was your age. You know, stories about what a good boy I was. I never fought. I never talked back. I always did what my parents told me…"

"OK, now, I'm off to my meeting. NO, you can't come with me. OK, now before I leave, say 'Goodbye' and also 'Thank you' and 'I'm sorry' and 'Excuse me' too! Little Mommy, I'm going to pick you up and throw you in the air! I'll let go and see if you can fly! Why are you crying? Don't you get the joke? Okay, little Daddy, a nice big wet kiss on the forehead for you! And little Mommy, a nice tight pinch on the cheek for you just like Aunt Marcia does. Now little Mommy, are you sad because you think I love little Daddy more than you? I love both of you equally! Little Daddy, get away from my chair! And be nice to your sister!"

On and on went Matthew's game, a game in which the parents were the children and the children were the parents. They might have played like this for days, but the football game was on. And the chicken was in the oven. And the phone rang for Mommy. "OK, that's enough!" Daddy announced. "I need my chair back for the game."

"Yes," Mommy agreed, "and it's just about time for bed, so off you go!"

Daddy Matthew became plain old Matthew again, and Mommy Amy was once again little baby Amy. Daddy watched the game.

Mommy talked on the phone. And the kids went to bed and slept very well. Just as they always did. Except for one thing. When Daddy and Mommy went to bed, they thought about Matthew and Amy's game. Maybe tomorrow, they thought, we won't say no so much. Tomorrow things will be different.

Parent and Teacher EQ Guide

 ## Inside the Talking Treasure

Every young child secretly (or not so secretly) wants to be able to give his or her parents orders, tell them where to go and what they can and cannot do, and what their bedtime should be. Sometimes, young children can feel very powerless to change the rules of the house. This story takes these feelings and puts them into words. In the story's game, children get their chance to be the parents, and the parents have to work at being children. But it's not so easy being in charge; rules can help children feel secure. In addition, through the game, the parents have a better understanding of how they treat their children.

The message for parents and teachers is that children may complain, but they benefit from having regular routines and schedules. Children also benefit, though, from having their feelings considered instead of simply being ordered around. Many children also notice that Matthew is a very good observer. He is brave, has an excellent imagination, and is able to voice his talking treasure by playing make believe. For parents, another lesson may be to think about how even well-intentioned actions affect children's feelings. Too much freedom can be as scary for young children as too little.

 ## Exploring the Talking Treasure

1. Was Matthew really the Daddy?

2. Why did Matthew decide he was going to be Daddy and his little sister Amy would be Mommy?

3. How did Daddy and Mommy feel about Matthew being in charge? How did little Amy feel about what was happening?

4. When Matthew was the Daddy, did he have fun? When the parents were the children, did they have fun?

5. Whose idea was it to stop the game? Why did they stop?

6. What are all the different feelings you think Matthew had when he was the Daddy?

7. What is the talking treasure that is inside of Matthew that makes him so special?

 ## Spreading the Talking Treasure

1. Take out some puppets and tell the story with members of your family or class acting the different parts.

2. Notice how you ask your child to do chores and carry out responsibilities. See if you can do it more often in ways that take your child's feelings into consideration.

3. When your child asks you a question, how do you answer? Do you take the time to explain as well as give an answer? Are there meetings you can take your child to or tell your child more about before you leave and after you come back? If you can do these things more often, your child will feel more respected and more a part of your life.

4. Go through some family picture albums with your child and explain who various relatives are. Children enjoy learning about the mommies, daddies, grandparents, and great-grandparents in their families.

5. Have everyone in the family write or draw something with the title "What Being in This Family Means to Me." Another possible title is "What Is Special and Good About Our Family?" Sometimes families do this by making a family coat of arms or by dividing a page into quarters and having each person write or draw four things. Or everyone in the family can work together to plan one set of responses that everyone can agree upon. This activity is a good way to let all members share a little bit of their talking treasure about the family.

Appendix

What Is "EQ"—Emotionally Intelligent Parenting and Teaching?

Emotional intelligence—or "EQ"—is something very important for our children and students. It is another way of being smart. For success in life, our children need to be able to use their heads and their hearts equally well.

Every day, trying to be citizens of one's community, classroom, and family brings with it dilemmas and decisions for which the skills of emotional intelligence need to be mobilized. Many of these skills, and the moral sensitivity to know when and how to use them, can be developed through the use of the stories in this book.

It's a Difficult Time to Be a Child

This is a very difficult time to be a child. There are more influences than ever on children, along with more sources of distraction. As psychiatrist and educator James Comer pointed out, never before in human history has there been so much information going directly to children, unfiltered by adult caregivers. The late Cornell child development specialist Uri Bronfenbrenner made a similar observation that we are in the age of "hecticness"; we are busy planning how to get children to where they have to be next, to get ourselves where we have to be, rushing from things to thing, wondering if all of our arrangements will work out.

The reality is, for some children, that life is harsh and unsafe; for others, it is packed with tension. In either case, losing emotional control can mean loss of privileges, loss of after-school or mentoring activities, or even placement in special school settings or living arrangements. Children need to grow up with opportunities in a positive, nurturing environment. Reading stories with themes relating to emotional intelligence to young children, especially between the ages of four and eight, when their language skills are blossoming, will create an opportunity for optimal growth in this area.

What Emotional Intelligence Is... and What It Is Not

Parenting or teaching with emotional intelligence is not something we do "by-the-numbers." Detailed, step-by-step approaches—"five weeks to a new household," "seven steps to better-behaved children," "how to become the model parent or teacher," and the like—look good on paper and sound inviting when authors and experts talk about them. But these types of approaches rarely seem to work in *your* home or classroom. We want to emphasize that this is not your failing. It is because emotionally intelligent parenting and teaching is a mix of many different things; it involves actions that help create a healthier balance in households and classrooms and in parents, teachers, and relationships with children.

Amidst all this stress, however, there is some relief. The basics of human biology, childrearing, teaching, and caregiver-child relationships have not changed. And this is what we must not lose sight of. Daniel Goleman's worldwide best-selling book, *Emotional Intelligence*, along with David Brooks' more recent bestseller, *The Social Animal*, when properly understood, have as their main point that we have neglected the biology of our feelings as adults and the role of feelings in our children's healthy growth. We are now paying for this, as families, schools, and as a society. We are paying by higher incidence of violence and disrespectful behavior. We are paying when we emphasize the intellect of students but forget their hearts. And, of course, our children pay as well, as indications of their un-happiness and troubled behaviors continue to rise.

Building Blocks of Emotional Intelligence

What exactly is emotional intelligence? The complex answer is that it is the ability to understand, manage, and express our feelings, thoughts, and actions in ways that help us manage everyday life tasks, such as learning, forming relationships, solving problems, and making choices. The specific skills involved include self-awareness, control of impulsivity, working cooperatively, and caring about oneself and others. The simple answer is "It's a different way of being smart."

Our society needs thinking, feeling, and capable citizens, workers, parents, and leaders. What can be done to help children grow up emotionally healthy? A great deal of work, much of it research, has addressed this issue. Over the past decades, groups such as the Consortium on the School-Based Promotion of Social Competence, the Collaborative for Academic, Social, and Emotional Learning, the Association for Supervision and Curriculum Development, the National Association of School Psychologists, and the Character Education Partnership all agree on the importance of helping children improve their social and emotional skills.

The stories in this book present lessons that will help children learn what they need to leap over the hurdles that life puts in their way. Specifically, they provide the following building blocks of emotional intelligence:

▪ **Emotional awareness**—Relationships are based on being able to accurately identify emotions in oneself and others.

▪ **Confidence**—Having a willingness to try new things and take prudent risks comes from a belief that success in one's activities is likely and that adults can be helpful.

▪ **Curiosity**—Asking questions and exploring and expanding our capacities and knowledge is a source of happiness and satisfaction in life.

▪ **Goal-directedness**—Our actions have meaning, purpose, and a positive impact on the world around us; what we do matters in ways we cannot always be aware of.

▪ **Appreciation and specialness**—We should not take what we have, or are given, for granted; it is not only important to feel a sense of appreciation but also to express our appreciation to others for the small and large things they do for us; in the same way, it is important to appreciate our own value and special qualities.

▪ **Self-discipline**—We are not governed by our impulses but can refine and make choices about our actions, manage anger, and tolerate teasing and other forms of frustration. Even when we cannot control how we are feeling in difficult times, we are still responsible for our actions and need to learn how to make healthy and constructive choices.

▪ **Empathy**—We have the capacity to understand others' perspectives, ideas, and feelings through verbal and nonverbal means, and this allows us to exchange ideas, feelings, and experiences with others.

▪ **Cooperation**—To be truly effective and happy in the world, it is important to create a balance of one's own and others' needs within families, teams, schools, and other groups.

Teaching and Parenting with EQ

Teaching and parenting with emotional intelligence consist of specific, simple, important techniques that can make a difference in household and classroom peace and harmony. These techniques all have been developed from hands-on work that the authors conduct daily with parents, families, and schools. This type of parenting and teaching is based on adults' working with their own and children's emotions in intelligent, constructive, positive, and creative ways, respecting biological reality and the role of feelings in human nature. It draws its strength from small changes in our relationships with children that are repeated day after day. A major goal of parenting and teaching with emotional intelligence is to lessen stress and add more fun into time spent with children.

The lessons of emotionally intelligent parenting and teaching are best taught through everyday family situations, such as bedtimes, meal times, car times, and school-related times. In the classroom, they are often conveyed during circle times, health classes, social studies, and group guidance and character education periods. And what better way to share these lessons with children than through stories? A story a day can improve the health of your relationships with children. The questions and activities deepen these effects. For optimal relationship health, read them again and again!

Story Sources

The stories in this book came together from a variety of sources. Each has evolved and changed to become the one it is today through a chain of telling and retelling. Story sources include the following:

1—*The Talking Treasure: Expressing One's Inner Feelings*

An original story by Vered Hankin. It is based on the principles of mindfulness, paying attention to what one experiences in the moment, and allowing whatever is present to be there just as it is. A spark of this story was originally inspired by a storytelling jam with *Golems of Gotham* author Thane Rosenbaum (Perennial/Harper Collins, 2003).

2—*The Horse Who Thought She Was a Puppy: A New Family Member Arrives*

This tale originated as a Greek fable. The 2nd century Greek writer Lucian alluded to the story in his play *Timon the Misanthrope.* A version is also referred to in the gospel of Thomas, in which Jesus is quoted as saying, "Woe to the Pharisees, for they are like a dog sleeping in the manger of oxen, for neither does he eat nor does he let the oxen eat." The tale has evolved a great deal since then. In this version, by Vered Hankin, the story serves as a jumping off point for discussing sibling rivalry.

3—*The Four-Eyed King: Overcoming a Disability*

Originally conceived by Devorah Omer (in *Voice of the Heart*, Joseph Srebrek, Israel, 2003). This version is retold by Vered Hankin.

4—*The Apple Tree's Wish: The Beauty Within*

Retold by Vered Hankin, based on "The Apple Tree's Discovery," by Peninnah Schram and Rachayl Eckstein Davis. A version of their story appears in the anthology *Chosen Tales*, edited by Peninnah Schram, published by Jason Aronson, an imprint of Rowman & Littlefield, © 1995; "Apples and Pomegranates," by Rahel Musleah, Kar-Ben Publishing © 2005; and "The Apple Tree's Discovery," by Peninnah Schram and Rachayl Eckstein Davis, Kar-Ben Publishing © 2012. Peninnah and Rachayl first heard the story at a midrash workshop taught by Rabbi Avi Weiss in the first Jewish Storytelling Festival (New York City, 1984). According to Rabbi Weiss, the story is probably a Chinese parable, reminding us of the beauty and potential we all have within. The story also highlights the magic and hidden gifts of the natural world.

5—*The Girl Who Never Lost: Taking Risks*

An original story by Devorah Omer (in *Voice of the Heart*, Joseph Srebrek, Israel 2002), translated by Vered Hankin.

6—*The Reed and the Wind: Strength in Flexibility*

"The Oak and the Reed," as it was originally called, is one of Aesop's fables (#70 in the Perry index of Aesop's fables). It was quoted later in the Jewish book of laws, the Talmud (Babylonian Talmud, 20a). In the Talmud, Rabbi Simeon ben Elazar alludes to the story by saying that a person should "be pliable like a reed, not rigid like a cedar." In this version by Vered Hankin, this theme is explored through the characters' lens.

7—When Mr. Pot Cracked: The Beauty of Imperfection

Story retold by Vered Hankin. Based on a folktale relayed by storyteller Nitzan Sitzer.

8—The Night the Toys Were Left Alone: Dealing with Separation

An original story by Devorah Omer (in *The Kiss that Got Lost*, Joseph Srebrek, Israel, 1978), translated by Vered Hankin.

9—David and the Spider: Everyone Has Value

A retelling of a classic midrash, a Jewish oral tradition of interpretations based on the Bible. It was originally written in the medieval Hebrew work the *Alphabet of Ben Sirah*. The story has been told many times since then in a multitude of modern versions, all illustrating the theme of the importance of all living creatures.

10—The Day the Children Became the Parents: Developing Empathy and Appreciation

An original story by Devorah Omer (in *The Kiss that Got Lost*, Joseph Srebrek, Israel, 1978), translated by Vered Hankin.

About the Authors

Vered Hankin, Ph.D., is a clinical psychologist and internationally acclaimed storyteller. As both psychologist and storyteller, Vered lectures and performs nationally and internationally in venues as diverse as academic conferences, theaters, charitable organizations, and radio and television. She has been named "the leading storyteller of her generation" (Howard Schwartz, *The Jewish Week*). Her publications include stories and essays in *On the Fringes: An Anthology of Young Jewish Women's Writings* (SUNY Press, 2003), *The Complete Guide to Storytelling for Parents* (Norton Press, 2000), and interviews in such publications as *Response and New Voices*. Vered's CD recording, *The Day the Rabbi Disappeared: Jewish Holiday Tales of Magic,* based on Howard Schwartz's National Jewish Book Award–winning collection, was produced by Broadway producer Shari Upbin. The CD received the prestigious Award of Excellence from the Film Advisory Board, as well as The Gold Award from NAPPA (National Association of Parenting Publication Awards). In addition, Vered joined celebrities Jerry Stiller, Leonard Nimoy, and Henry Winkler in an internationally aired radio show and audio CD of children's folktales, *One People: Many Stories.* In addition to her storytelling escapades, Vered is Research Assistant Professor at the Department of Medical Social Sciences at Northwestern University. She is also founder and director of MBSR Chicago, an organization devoted to mindfulness interventions for chronic illness. She lives in Chicago with her husband, Jeremy Kaufman, and their two children, Jonah and Coral.

Devorah Omer was born on Kibbutz Maoz Haim in 1932. She completed her studies in 1952 and became a teacher. In addition to writing and adapting more than 100 books for children and youth, she has written plays, radio scripts, a novel for adults, and personal columns in several children's magazines. One of the most prolific and popular children's writers in Israel, Devorah has received many awards, including the Yatziv Prize (1959), the Lamdan Prize (1967, 1981), the Ministry of Education Prize (1973), the Prime Minister's Prize (1979), an Andersen International Honor Citation (1986), the Ze'ev Prize (1981, 1991), the Janusz Korczak Medal (1987), the Hadassah Prize (2002), the Ministry of Education Prize for Lifetime Achievement (2005), and the Israel Prize for Lifetime Achievement (2006).

Maurice J. Elias, Ph.D., is a professor and director of clinical training in the Psychology Department at Rutgers University. He also serves as academic director for Rutgers' Civic Engagement and Service Education Partnerships Program (CESEP); Coordinator of Rutgers' Internship Program in Applied, School, and Community Psychology; director of Rutgers' Social-Emotional Learning Lab; and Coordinator of Improving School Climate for Academic and Life Success (ISCALS) at Rutgers' Center for Applied Psychology. A past president of the International Society for Community Research and Action/Division of Community Psychology (Division 27) of the American Psychological Association and a founding member of the leadership team for the Collaborative for Academic, Social, and Emotional Learning (CASEL), Maurice is also a past winner of the Lela Rowland Prevention Award, the Ernest McMahon Class of 1930 Award for service to New Jersey, and the APA/Society for Community Research and Action's Distinguished Contribution to Practice and Ethnic Minority Mentoring awards. Maurice lectures nationally and internationally, has been featured on numerous television and radio programs, and has written an award-winning weekly parenting column, most recently for the Sunday *Newark Star-Ledger*. He is author or co-author of *Emotionally Intelligent Parenting* (Three Rivers Press), the *Social Decision Making/Social Problem Solving* curricula for elementary and middle school students (Research Press), *The Educator's Guide to Emotional Intelligence and Academic Achievement* (Corwin), *Bullying, Victimization, and Peer Harassment* (Taylor & Francis), *Urban Dreams: Stories of Hope, Character, and Resilience* (Hamilton Books), and *School Climate: Building Safe, Supportive, and Engaging Classrooms and Schools* (National Professional Resources). His most recent work is the e-book *Emotionally Intelligent Parenting* (available from www.amazon.com and www.barnesandnoble.com). Maurice also writes a blog on social-emotional and character development (SECD) for the George Lucas Educational Foundation. He is married and has two daughters and a new grandson, Harry Elijah Stopek, to whom he has already started to read the stories in this book.

Amiram Raviv, Ph.D., is a school and clinical psychologist. He is dean of the School of Psychology at The Center for Academic Studies at Or Yehuda Israel and professor emeritus at the Psychology Department, Tel Aviv University, where he has served as department chair. Amiram is co-author of the Hebrew books *Crisis and Change in the Life of the Child and His/Her Family*, *The Israeli Parents' Guide*, and *Grandparenting Today*, as well as co-editor of *Peace, Conflict and War: International Perspectives on the Development of Their Understanding by Children and Adolescents*, published in English. He has also published over 100 articles and chapters in professional journals and books. In addition to his academic pursuits, he has been active in various areas of primary prevention, serving as consultant for a number of parenting websites and children's books. The latter include the best-selling books *Pyramid of Blocks* and *The Kiss That Got Lost*, written by award-winning Israeli author Devorah Omer. Recently, Amiram and Maurice Elias collaborated in the development of and commentary for Devorah Omer's *Voice of the Heart*, an Israeli storybook promoting emotional intelligence. Amiram has also written and served as consultant for numerous enrichment programs for toddlers and kindergarten-age children, as well as guidance literature for parents, for a total of 20 books and three book series. He served for more than 15 years as a consultant for the Israeli Educational Television Network on various programs providing counseling to parents. He is married, with two daughters and five grandchildren.